Palaces

Macdonald Educational

workers

Long ago there were no machines.
Building a palace was hard work.
Many workers moved the heavy stones.
2

craftsmen

Craftsmen decorated the palace.
Each man had a special job.
Some carved the stone
and others painted it.

3

Brighton Pavilion, England

Tsarskoe Selo, Russia

Burg Eltz an der Mosel, Germany

Linderhof Palace, Germany

Here are some palaces.
They are in different countries.
Some palaces are very old.
You can still visit their ruins today.

4

In China palaces had beautiful gardens.
This garden belonged to the Emperor.
Workers made hills and dug lakes.
They built bridges over the lakes.

Many palaces had a theatre.
Sometimes the theatre was built in the garden.
The king and his friends
watched plays and dances there.

6

People who lived in palaces
often went falconing.
A falcon is a hunting bird.
It hunts other birds and kills them in the air.
Dogs went to find the dead birds.

This is a huge palace in France.
It is the Palace of Versailles.
Later it was made even bigger than this.
8

Versailles was built for a French king.
People called him the Sun King.

Ladies who lived in palaces wore
beautiful clothes with small waists.
They took a long time to dress and
they had many maids to help them.

10

Many people worked in palaces.
They got up early in the morning.
They lit the fires
and cleaned the rooms.

coachmen

groom

kennel boy

gamekeeper   gardener

These men had jobs outside.
The groom looked after the horses.
The kennel boy fed the hounds.

12

The cooks are preparing a meal.
They roast the meat on a spit.

Often it was a long way
from the kitchen to the dining room.
The servants had to hurry
in case the food got cold.

chandelier

People at the palace
ate in the banqueting hall.
A banquet was a big feast.
People ate a lot at banquets.

15

This is the Empress Josephine.
Her bed had beautiful curtains.
They helped to keep out the cold.

Here is the sultan's palace in Turkey.
A sultan is a king.
All these girls looked after the sultan.

17

chandelier

musicians

This is a fancy dress ball long ago.
Everybody dressed up.
Some people wore masks.

18

footman

Travelling musicians and performers
came to play.
All the people liked to dance.

Many palaces had a maze in the garden.
Tall thick hedges made a puzzle.
You had to find the right path out.

embroidery

A teacher lived at the palace.
The boys had many lessons.
Girls did not do so many lessons.
They learnt to sew and embroider instead.

The Pope lives at the Vatican Palace
in Rome.
The Pope is the head
of the Roman Catholic Church.

A new Pope is chosen by the Cardinals.
The crowd waits to hear the news.
When they see the white smoke
they know a Pope has been chosen.

Queen Victoria is opening
the Crystal Palace.
It was built in Hyde Park.
It was like a giant green house.
Nobody lived there.
24

Many people visited the Crystal Palace.
They came to see the Great Exhibition.
People sent things from all over the world.
This palace was moved to Sydenham.
Later it burnt down.

25

You can make a chandelier like this.
Use card and kitchen foil.
It will glitter like a real one.
26

Try and make up a maze game.
Play it with your friends.
Who is the first to find the way out?

27

Index